DISCOVERING THE UNITED STATES

North Dakota

BY YVETTE LaPIERRE

Kids Core
An Imprint of Abdo Publishing
abdobooks.com

abdobooks.com

Printed in China.
052024
092024

Cover Photo: Brian A. Wolf/Shutterstock Images
Interior Photos: Nawrocki/ClassicStock/Archive Photos/Getty Images, 4–5; Franz Marc Frei/The Image Bank Unreleased/Getty Images, 7; Whitney Schwab/Shutterstock Images, 9; Brian Lasenby/Shutterstock Images, 10 (top left); iStockphoto, 10 (top right); Anzhela Shvab/Shutterstock Images, 10 (bottom left); Shutterstock Images, 10 (bottom right), 16; North Wind Picture Archives/Alamy, 12–13; Frilet Patrick/Hemis/Alamy, 15; Manu Padilla/Shutterstock Images, 18; Jacob Boomsma/Shutterstock Images, 20–21, 28 (top right), 29 (bottom); Guy William/Shutterstock Images, 22, 28 (bottom); Peter Elvin/Alamy, 23; Life Atlas Photography/Shutterstock Images, 25; Tracy Kerestesh/Shutterstock Images, 26; Red Line Editorial, 28 (top left), 29 (top)

Editor: Haley Williams
Series Designer: Katharine Hale

Library of Congress Control Number: 2023949362

Publisher's Cataloging-in-Publication Data

Names: LaPierre, Yvette, author.
Title: North Dakota / by Yvette LaPierre
Description: Minneapolis, Minnesota: Abdo Publishing, 2025 | Series: Discovering the United States | Includes online resources and index.
Identifiers: ISBN 9781098294045 (lib. bdg.) | ISBN 9798384913313 (ebook)
Subjects: LCSH: U.S. states--Juvenile literature. | North Dakota--History--Juvenile literature. | Midwest States--Juvenile literature. | Physical geography--United States--Juvenile literature.
Classification: DDC 973--dc23

All population data taken from:
"Estimates of Population by Sex, Race, and Hispanic Origin: April 1, 2020 to July 1, 2022." *US Census Bureau, Population Division*, June 2023, census.gov.

CONTENTS

Meriwether Lewis and William Clark traveled about 8,000 miles (12,900 km) across the United States between 1804 and 1806.

CHAPTER 1

The Bird Woman

It was a fall day in 1804. Five Mandan and Hidatsa American Indian villages sat on the **bluffs** along the Missouri River in North Dakota. Two white men arrived at the villages by boat. Their names were Meriwether Lewis and William Clark.

The American Indian peoples welcomed Lewis and Clark. They also listened to the men's story. Lewis and Clark had traveled from Missouri. They were on a journey to explore the land out West.

While at the villages, the explorers met a French fur trader. They also met the fur trader's young Shoshone wife. Her name was Sakakawea (Sacagawea). This meant "Bird Woman."

Sakakawea joined Lewis and Clark on their journey. She helped the explorers communicate with other American Indian people. Today, a statue of Sakakawea stands in North Dakota. It honors her importance during the Lewis and Clark **Expedition**.

Statues of Sakakawea sometimes show her with her baby. She carried her son on her back while traveling thousands of miles with Lewis and Clark.

North Dakota's Land

North Dakota is located in the US Midwest region. Minnesota borders North Dakota to the east. South Dakota is to the south, and Montana is to the west. To the north is Canada. North Dakota is named after the Dakota American Indian people. *Dakota* means "friend" or "ally."

North Dakota has many different landscapes. The Red River Valley in the east is flat farmland.

North America's Center

Rugby, North Dakota, is known as the geographic center of North America. This means it is the centermost point of North America when measured from east to west and north to south. People can visit a stone monument that marks the spot.

White Butte is the highest point in North Dakota. It is 3,506 feet (1,069 m) above sea level.

In the middle of the state is the Drift Prairie region. Small lakes and ponds are found throughout the area. In the far west is the Missouri Plateau. The rocky **buttes** and colorful canyons of this area are known as the Badlands.

North Dakota Facts

DATE OF STATEHOOD
November 2, 1889

CAPITAL
Bismarck

POPULATION
779,261

AREA
70,698 square miles (183,107 sq km)

STATE BIRD

Western meadowlark

STATE TREE

American elm

STATE FLOWER

Wild prairie rose

STATE HORSE

Nokota horse

Each US state has a different population, size, and capital city. States also have state symbols.

Many animals call North Dakota home. American bison can be found in Theodore Roosevelt National Park. Other animals in North Dakota include moose, elk, bald eagles, and pronghorns.

North Dakota's Climate

North Dakota is mostly dry and sunny. It has four seasons. Summers tend to be warm and dry. July is the warmest month. Winters in the state are long, cold, and snowy. The coldest month is January. Temperatures can often be 0 degrees Fahrenheit (−18°C) or colder.

Further Evidence

Look at the website below. Does it give any new information about North Dakota?

North Dakota

abdocorelibrary.com/discovering-north-dakota

The Mandan, Hidatsa, and Arikara nations in North Dakota lived in homes called earth lodges. The lodges were made from wood and grasses.

The People of North Dakota

The first American Indians arrived in North Dakota about 13,000 years ago. Many **descendants** of these people continue to live in the state today. North Dakota has five federally recognized tribes.

These include the Spirit Lake Nation and Standing Rock Sioux Tribe.

The first white explorers arrived in North Dakota in the 1700s and 1800s. The most famous were Lewis and Clark. In the late 1800s, many **immigrants** arrived in the state. Most were from Germany, Norway, Finland, Sweden, and Denmark. The **settlers** built homes and towns close to main railroads.

In 2022, fewer than 780,000 people lived in North Dakota. It has one of the lowest populations of any US state. White people made up 83 percent of the population. About 5 percent of North Dakotans were American Indian. Another 5 percent of people were Hispanic or Latino. And 4 percent were Black.

More than 37,000 American Indian people live in North Dakota today. Many honor their cultures by dancing and wearing traditional clothing.

Culture

North Dakota's American Indian peoples have shaped the state's culture. One of the nation's biggest American Indian **powwows** is held in Bismarck, North Dakota. The United Tribes Powwow celebrates American Indian culture.

North Dakota's state flag features 13 stars, which stand for the first 13 states in the United States.

People hold dancing and drumming contests during the celebration.

Food is another important part of North Dakota's culture. Potatoes are used in many popular dishes in the state. Tater Tot hot dish is a casserole made with Tater Tots and ground beef. Lefse is a Norwegian potato flatbread. Potato chips dipped in chocolate are known as chippers.

In North Dakota, many people enjoy the outdoors year-round. Popular winter activities include skiing, snowmobiling, and ice fishing. In the summer, hiking, biking, and camping are popular activities throughout the state's parks.

French Fry Record

Grand Forks, North Dakota, holds the world's largest french fry feed every year. In 2017, hundreds of people came together during the city's Potato Bowl festival. They ate more than 8,000 pounds (3,600 kg) of fries. This set a new festival record.

North Dakota produces more honey than any other US state.

Industry

Agriculture is the leading industry in North Dakota. The state has almost 26,000 farms and ranches. North Dakota farmers lead the nation in producing many foods, including dry beans, wheat, and honey. Farmers in the state also grow potatoes.

Many people in North Dakota also have jobs in the energy industry. The state is a top producer of oil, gas, and coal. It also produces a lot of wind and solar energy.

In 2023, the United Tribes Powwow was held at United Tribes Technical College. Brent Kleinjan, who worked at the college, talked about the importance of the powwow:

> [The Powwow is] a great way for the community, even those who aren't Native Americans themselves, to learn about the culture.

Source: Brendan Rodenberg. "Weekend BRB: United Tribes Powwow 2023." *KX News*, 10 Sept. 2023, kxnet.com. Accessed 1 Jan. 2024.

What's the Big Idea?

Read this quote carefully. What is its main idea? Explain how the main idea is supported by details.

Fargo sits along the Red River of the North on the border between North Dakota and Minnesota.

Places in North Dakota

Bismarck is the capital of North Dakota. It sits along the Missouri River in the south-central part of the state. Fargo is the state's largest city by population. Grand Forks is another big city. The University of North Dakota is there.

Theodore Roosevelt National Park covers more than 70,400 acres (28,490 ha) across three areas of land in North Dakota.

Parks and Landmarks

North Dakota has many places to visit. Theodore Roosevelt National Park is the only national park in the state. It is named after former president Theodore Roosevelt. He visited the

Today, people can go inside the reconstructed earth lodges at the Knife River Indian Villages National Historic Site to see what they looked like.

state in the 1880s. The park is found in the rocky badlands of western North Dakota. Visitors can see wildlife and hike on trails in the park.

Knife River Indian Villages National Historic Site is another important park. It includes the American Indian villages visited by Lewis and Clark. The Lewis and Clark Interpretive Center tells the story of the explorers in North Dakota.

Fort Totten State Historic Site was built in 1867. It was used as a military fort. During the late 1800s to mid-1900s, the fort was also used as a school and hospital. Fort Totten officially became a state historic site in 1960. Today, people can visit the museum there.

The International Peace Garden stands on the border between North Dakota and Canada.

Big Bison

Jamestown, North Dakota, has the world's largest bison statue. It stands 26 feet (8 m) tall and is made of concrete. The statue is located near the National Buffalo Museum. In 2010, a contest was held to name the bison. It was named Dakota Thunder.

Many people enjoy fishing, boating, and kayaking on Lake Sakakawea.

More than 155,000 flowers bloom there. The garden represents the friendship between the United States and Canada.

Bison calves are born in the spring. About that time of year, bison also shed their thick winter coats.

North Dakota also has 63 national wildlife refuges. That is the most of any state. Refuges are areas that protect important habitats and species. The North American bison is found in several protected places throughout the state.

There are many things people can do in North Dakota. They can learn about the state's American Indian culture or visit different parks and historic sites. And they can enjoy skiing, hiking, and camping. North Dakota has something to offer everyone.

Explore Online

Visit the website below. Does it give you any new information about Theodore Roosevelt National Park that wasn't in Chapter Three?

Theodore Roosevelt National Park

abdocorelibrary.com/discovering-north-dakota

State Map

KEY

 Capital

Park

City or town

 Point of interest

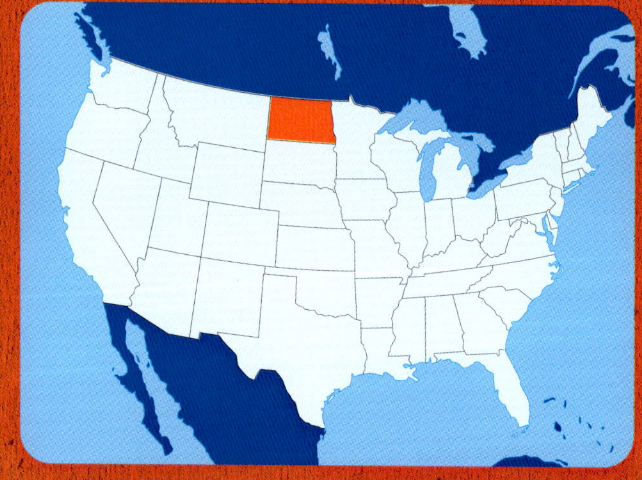

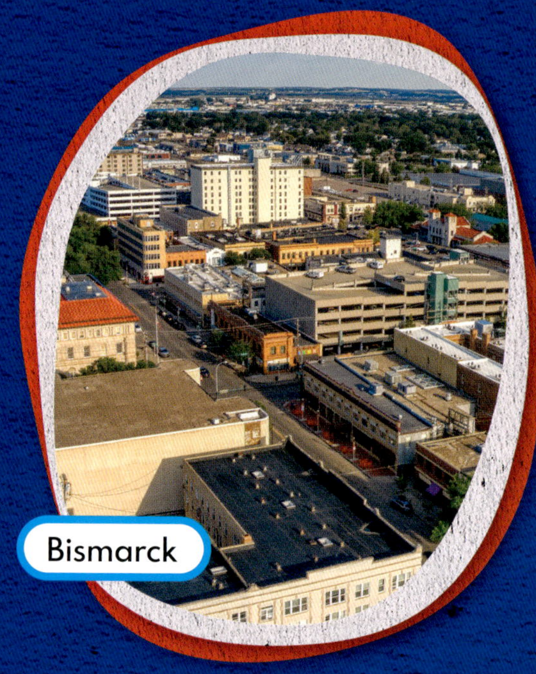

Bismarck

Theodore Roosevelt National Park

North Dakota: The Peace Garden State

CANADA

International Peace Garden

Rugby

Missouri River

Fort Union Trading Post National Historic Site

Lake Sakakawea

Devils Lake

University of North Dakota

Grand Forks

Fort Totten State Historic Site

Lewis and Clark Interpretive Center

Montana

Minnesota

Knife River Indian Villages National Historic Site

Theodore Roosevelt National Park

Jamestown

Fargo

Bismarck

White Butte

South Dakota

International Peace Garden

Glossary

bluffs
steep hills, cliffs, or banks

buttes
hills with steep sides and flat tops

descendants
people who are related to a person or group that lived in the past

expedition
a journey taken by a group of people for a purpose, such as exploration or research

immigrants
people who move to a different country

powwow
a celebration honoring American Indian culture that includes singing, dancing, and feasting

settlers
people who moved to a new area

Online Resources

To learn more about North Dakota, visit our free resource websites below.

Visit **abdocorelibrary.com** or scan this QR code for free Common Core resources for teachers and students, including vetted activities, multimedia, and booklinks, for deeper subject comprehension.

Visit **abdobooklinks.com** or scan this QR code for free additional online weblinks for further learning. These links are routinely monitored and updated to provide the most current information available.

Learn More

Murray, Julie. *North Dakota.* Abdo, 2020.

Payne, Stefanie. *The National Parks: Discover All 62 National Parks of the United States.* DK, 2020.

Perdew, Laura. *Grassland Biomes.* Abdo, 2024.

Index

About the Author

Yvette LaPierre lives in North Dakota with her family and advises students in the Indians Into Medicine Program at the University of North Dakota. She has written more than 30 books for children.